M000290358

LEATHERCRAFT
FOR BEGINNERS
With Easy-to-Do Projects

ROSS C. CRAMLET

DOVER PUBLICATIONS, INC.
Mineola, New York

Bibliographical Note

This Dover edition, first published in 2006, is an unabridged republication of *Fundamentals of Leathercraft,* originally published by The Bruce Publishing Company, Milwaukee, in 1939.

International Standard Book Number: 0-486-45280-8

Manufactured in the United States of America
Dover Publications, Inc., 31 East 2nd Street, Mineola, N.Y. 11501

PREFACE

Leathercraft is receiving much attention in the schools and home workshops today. The art of making useful articles from leather is truly fascinating, and may easily establish itself as a permanent interest with many persons. It offers unlimited possibilities in the field of design and in artistic self-expression.

It has been found by those who do the work to be exceedingly practical. A moment's thought will recall the fact that every man, woman, and child has need for and uses articles of leather in the common activities of daily life. What person does not use a belt, a pocketbook, key case, handbag, or some other common article made of leather?

The main purpose of this book is to give fundamental information and instruction to the beginner in leatherwork, placing emphasis upon the types of materials to be selected for different articles, and the simple tool processes necessary to make things desired.

CONTENTS

STORY OF LEATHER

When the first Colonists came to America, they were much surprised to find that the inhabitants of this continent were tanning animal hides and skins. It is not known exactly where this knowledge, as used by the Red Man, came from. However, it was readily observable that the Indians possessed uncommon skill in preparing the hides and skins for use as clothing and shelter, and for decoration.

The finest work of tanning, by the Indians at that time, was demonstrated on buckskins. They used wood ashes for removing the hair. Crude pieces of bone, stones, or shells, with a sharpened edge, were then employed for scraping and cleaning the hides. Rounded pieces of stone were used for rubbing in the tanning solution. The final processes of softening and coloring were accomplished by hanging the hides in tents over fires made of rottenwood. This cured and made the hides pliable and soft after they were dampened with water.

Today, many different chemicals are used in the modern tanning processes. The most common ones are saltpeter, common salt, Glauber salt, alum, borax, lime, sulphuric acid, and solutions made with oak bark. Neat's-foot oil is commonly used for softening hides.

Some of the finest leather in the world is made in America. The hides used come from all parts of the Western hemisphere. The highest quality hides seem to be produced in cold climates because the cold temperatures cause nature to produce thick and tough skins. Classification of leather is based on two things; first, the kind of animal from which it comes, and second, the tanning process that is used.

The craftsman uses leather made from calfskins, cowhides, steer hides, sheepskins, and goatskins.

OBTAINING MATERIAL

It is very essential that a beginner in leathercraft should know how to obtain the proper kind of material. There are a number of different ways in which this may be done.

First, a hide may be purchased from a dealer in leathers, and from this hide the project may be cut according to the patterns which have been developed. In many cases, this is a very satisfactory and economical method if a large number of projects are to be made. However, if a person is just beginning and has had no experience in cutting leather, the waste is likely to be excessive.

Second, the patterns made of heavy paper may be sent directly to a firm that sells leather. The dealer then cuts out the material and sends it to the student, ready for use. Usually the price is determined on the basis of the measurement per square inch. There are a number of leather supply houses which furnish leather cut in this way.

The third method is to buy scrap leather by the pound from leather supply houses and use this material for beginners. It is questionable, however, whether the use of scrap leather is entirely satisfactory because these scraps are odd bits cut from the belly, flanks, and other thin parts of the hide. They are very soft and flimsy and extremely hard to work. Experience shows that buying the better grade of hide is usually the best in the end.

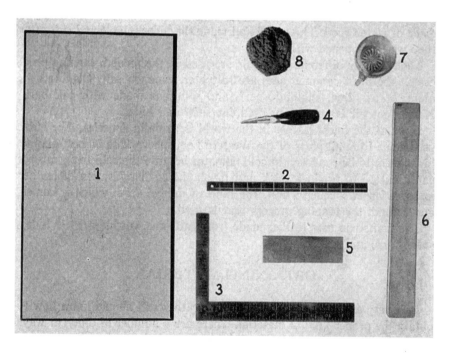

Fig. 1. Tools and equipment required for preparing the leather.

Material for linings may be obtained in the same way as the other leather needed for the different projects.

Material for lacing is very difficult to cut evenly in either the goatskin or calfskin lace, and it is usually the best plan to buy this material, cut ready for use, from a supply house. Lacing materials vary much in quality and oftentimes it is necessary to insist that supply houses furnish a better quality of material. Quality may be determined by the strength of the lace and the evenness with which it is cut. In no case should a good article be laced with material likely to break or wear in a short time.

TOOLS AND EQUIPMENT

In leatherwork, as in all other crafts, it is possible and many times convenient to have a large number of tools. After the beginner has progressed to the point where he is able to make the more difficult projects, he should be able to make and improvise different ways for doing things which will lessen the amount of equipment needed. The list of tools and materials recommended and described further on, has been limited to the smallest possible practical number. Figure 1 shows the materials needed for cutting and moistening the leather.

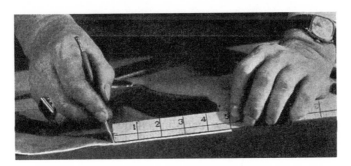

Fig. 2. Measuring with the rule.

1. CUTTING BOARD. A satisfactory cutting board for leatherwork is best made of softwood. Pine and bass are frequently used. A material which has a close grain is always better because the knife, when cutting through the leather, will not be drawn off its course by the irregular hardness of the grain. No. 1 in Figure 1, shows such a board.

2. RULE. The metal rule, shown as No. 2, in Figure 1, serves the twofold purpose of measuring, and, serving as a straightedge, is useful in

leatherwork. The proper way to use the rule for measuring is illustrated in Figure 2.

3. SMALL SQUARE. The small square shown as No. 3 in Figure 1, is of the framing-square type. It is the most convenient tool for insuring that leather is cut square. The method of holding the square and the relation of the knife to it are illustrated in Figure 3. It should be noted that the knife is held in such a position that the line of the blade is slanted out slightly from the edge of the square. If this is done the edge of the knife will follow the square better.

Fig. 3. Cutting a square piece of leather.

4. SHARP-POINTED KNIFE. The special type of sharp-pointed knife, shown as No. 4 in Figure 1, and also in Figure 4, is used for leatherwork. The length of the blade may be adjusted by loosening the handle and slipping the blade back and forth. When the knife is not in use, the blade

Fig. 4.

may be reversed and the sharp point recessed in the handle for protection. Only a small part of the blade should protrude from the handle when it is being used.

5. FAST-CUTTING WHETSTONE. A good whetstone is very necessary for leatherwork because, if the knife is not kept sharp, it will not make a

clean cut on the first stroke. Usually a second cut will not follow the original line, and a ragged edge will be left. The proper method of holding the stone and of whetting the knife is illustrated in Figure 5.

Fig. 5. Whetting the knife.

6. LEATHER STROP. A leather strop is used for removing the wire edge produced by the whetstone and for smoothing the cutting edge of the knife. A very satisfactory strop may be made by gluing a piece of cowhide to a soft pine board. The side is optional.

7. CONTAINER FOR WATER. A small container of glass or earthenware is necessary to hold the water with which the leather is moistened. A

Fig. 6. Moistening the leather.

Fig. 7. Using the metal rule as a straightedge.

metal can, which may rust, is not desirable, as light-colored leathers are readily ruined by rust spots or other discolorations.

8. SPONGE. A small, clean sponge is best for applying water to the surface of leather. The moistening process and the amount of moisture necessary are illustrated in Figure 6.

9. GLASS. For leather modeling a smooth, hard surface is necessary. A medium-sized piece of plate glass (an old automobile windshield will do) is well adapted for use as a modeling surface. A polished marble slab similarly offers an ideal surface for modeling processes.

10. STRAIGHTEDGE. Where straight-line indentations are to be made, a steel rule may be used as a straightedge to guide the various modeling

Fig. 8. Using the edge creaser.

tools. The rule should lie perfectly flat on the material. The proper method of using the rule as a straightedge is shown in Figure 7.

11. EDGE CREASER. Two types of edge creasers are in common use; one is made of metal, the other is a small piece of hardwood. The purpose of the tool is to crease the front of a flap or any exposed edges of leather such as are found in pocketbooks, coin purses, and the like. A wooden creaser works very satisfactorily under ordinary circumstances. Where a large amount of creasing is to be done, a metal creaser is more satisfactory. The metal creaser works better if heated a bit before it is used. The proper use of the edge creaser is illustrated in Figure 8.

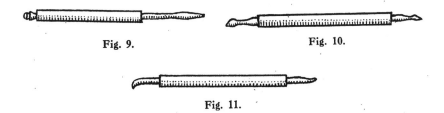

Fig. 9.   Fig. 10.

Fig. 11.

12. MODELERS. For all types of leather tooling, the modelers are the most important tools. They are used for beveling and burnishing outlines in outline creasing, for depressing and polishing backgrounds in flat modeling, and for raising the designs into relief in repoussé or embossing. A number of different shaped tools, all used for these processes, are

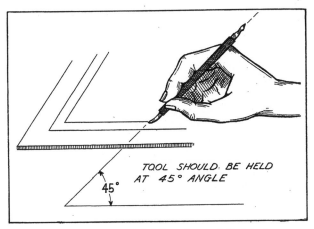

Fig. 12. Proper way of holding the modeling tool.

Fig. 13. Transferring the design from paper
pattern to leather.

classified as modelers. Three of the most common types of modelers are
shown in Figures 9, 10, and 11.

In order to do effective modeling, the modeler tool should be held at
an angle of approximately 45 deg. as shown in Figure 12. If the tool is
not held fairly erect, it will slip over the leather and will not make a
good indentation.

13. TRACER. Figure 9 shows the tracer. This is a pointed tool used

Fig. 14. Using the deerfoot in flat modeling.

Fig. 15. Stretching leather from the back with spadepoint.

for transferring the design from the paper pattern to the leather as shown in Figure 13. The tracer is also used to bring out the lines of a design after the pattern has been removed.

14. DEERFOOT. The deerfoot, shown in Figure 10, is used extensively in flat modeling. The shapes of its points are very suitable for developing almost any type of shaded effects. Figure 14 shows a typical deerfoot in use.

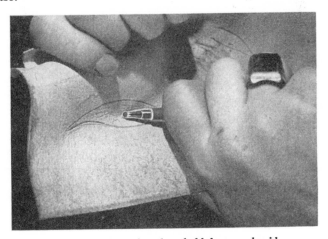

Fig. 16. Position of tool as held from underside.

15. SPADEPOINT. The spadepoint, shown in Figure 11, is extensively used for embossing, where stretching and raising of the leather is necessary. This is accomplished through pressure exerted from the underside, with the tip of the spadepoint tool as shown in Figures 15 and 16.

Fig. 17. Stippling the background.

16. STIPPLE OR BACKGROUND TOOL. The stipple tool is used for the development of a background which gives contrast to a design and makes certain desired lines stand out. Its use is comparatively simple. The stippling process is done over a piece of metal. In order to do nice work with the stipple tool, three things are necessary: the tool must be held perpendicular to the surface of the leather; uniform force must be applied to the blows of the mallet; and the tools should be struck squarely on the head. Figure 17 shows the proper way of using the stipple tool.

17. STAMPING TOOLS. Stamping tools are used for two general purposes; for the stamping of backgrounds and for the development of designs. When using the stamp, set it carefully in the exact spot wanted. Hold it as nearly perpendicular as possible, and strike it flat on the head with uniform force on each blow. See Figure 18.

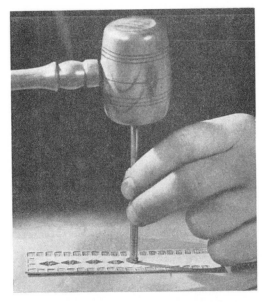

Fig. 18. Holding the stamp correctly.

Stamps are available in many different shapes. Seventeen common designs and a wood-block holder for a collection of stamps are shown in Figure 19.

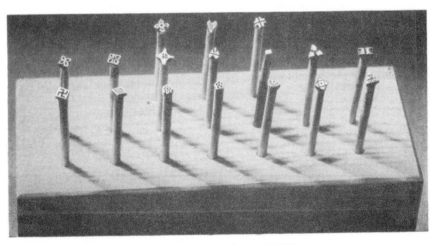

Fig. 19. Stamp design and holder.

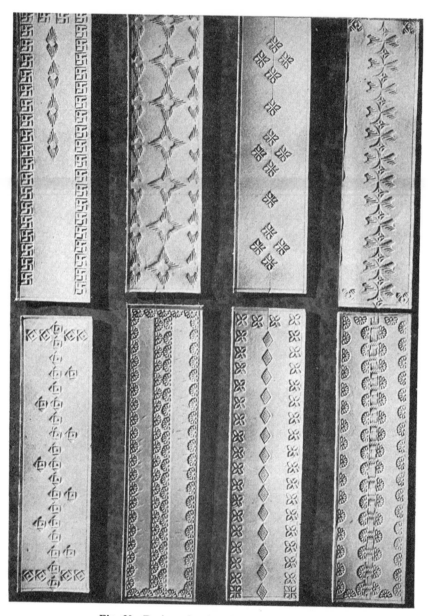

Fig. 20. Designs developed by use of stamps.

A few of the endless variety of designs which may be developed with the use of stamps, are shown in Figure 20.

18. STAMPING ANVIL. A heavy, smooth metal surface is needed upon which to do stamping. The base part of a flatiron, preferably of an electric iron, is ideal for this work. If this metal is nickel-plated, it is not so likely to discolor the leather. At any rate, no matter what kind of metal is used, be extremely careful to keep the working surface clean and free from oxidation so as not to discolor light materials.

19. MALLET. A hardwood mallet is used for stamping. This is done so that the upper end of the stamp is not battered up so much, and that the blows on the stamp are not so severe as to cause the tool to cut the surface of the leather rather than to indent it.

DESIGN

OBTAINING A DESIGN. Frequently the fear of not being able to make suitable designs deters the beginner from trying his hand at leatherwork. There are many things which may be suggested which will be helpful to individuals of this type. Good suggestions for designs, which may be adapted to leather articles, may be found in art magazines, leather catalogues, and in books on design.

If the individual does not have sufficient confidence in his own ability to develop designs, it might be advisable to give him a design already made. Many leather supply houses have sheets of suggested designs suitable for leather tooling.

SELECTING A GOOD DESIGN. In selecting a good design, the most important thing is simplicity of lines and detail. It is well to adapt the design to the article in such a way that the lines may be drawn with a rule, or by using curved objects which are available. The ability to do freehand line work with the tool will develop as the individual acquires experience in the use of leather-modeling tools.

MAKING A DESIGN. When the type of design suitable for the project has been selected, it should be developed in detail on a piece of durable paper to the exact size wanted. Every detail should be shown on the original pattern in order that, when it is transferred to the leather, it will present a complete guide in the tooling and modeling processes. The pattern should be made with a good drawing pencil.

PREPARING THE LEATHER FOR MODELING

MOISTENING THE LEATHER. Before the pattern can be transferred to the leather, the leather must be softened by applying moisture with a clean sponge. It is very necessary that the beginner should understand how to do this. No two pieces of leather can be prepared in the same manner because some skins will soften more easily than others. The leather should be softened until it will take an imprint when a reasonable amount of pressure is applied on the tracing tool. If the leather is moistened too much, it will be soft and flimsy and the imprint will disappear when the leather is handled. Neither will it retain the tooling processes which will be applied later. The method of applying moisture is illustrated in Figure 6.

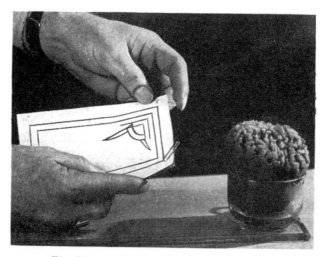

Fig. 21. Attaching paper pattern to leather.

TRANSFERRING THE DESIGN TO THE LEATHER. To transfer the design to the leather, the paper pattern which is the exact size of the leather that has been cut, should be fastened with paper clips. At least two or three clips should be used to make certain that the pattern will not slip until the entire imprint has been made. If it is necessary at any time to look at the leather to see whether the imprint is sufficiently deep, the pattern should remain fastened at one end, while it is lifted up at the other for making the inspection. This eliminates any possibility of its slipping. The proper method for attaching the pattern to the leather is illustrated in Figure 21.

The tool used for making the imprint is called a tracer. Use quite a bit of pressure on the tool while transferring the lines, as it will simplify the tooling process which will come later. The proper method for holding the tracing tool is shown in Figure 13.

METHODS OF DECORATING LEATHER

The processes of modeling leather have to do with the development of the design desired on its surface. It is fundamentally essential that the modeling processes be carefully studied and understood if good work is to be the result. The appearance of the final product is almost entirely dependent on the general effectiveness of the modeling and the lacing. For this reason, the learner should place emphasis on this part of the work.

Fig. 22. Flat modeling.

FLAT MODELING. There are two general methods of tooling leather. One is called *flat modeling* and the other is called *embossing*. The design usually determines the kind of modeling that is used. In flat modeling no part of the leather is raised above the original surface. A typical illustration of flat modeling is shown in Figure 22.

EMBOSSING. In this method of decoration, the design is brought in relief by raising it above the general surface. This is accomplished by working the design up from the underside. Sometimes it is recommended that the pattern should be traced on both sides of the leather. This is not generally necessary because the point of the tool can be located by the shadow on the leather. To make the contrast between surfaces more pronounced, other parts of the leather may be pressed down as in the case of flat modeling, which really involves a combination of two methods of modeling. Figure 23 is an illustration of embossing.

Fig. 23. Embossing.

METHODS OF ASSEMBLING

Lining

Most finished leather articles of better quality have linings of sheepskin, thin calfskin, goatskin, or antelope skin.

Suede linings, which are made from sheepskin, are very satisfactory for small purses, key cases, and articles of that type. But suede is not a practical lining for billfolds and larger articles because it will stretch with wear and will become. wrinkled.

Thin calf is very satisfactory for the lining of larger projects.

Antelope is used considerably and is a very high type of material for lining, but the cost is prohibitive in many instances.

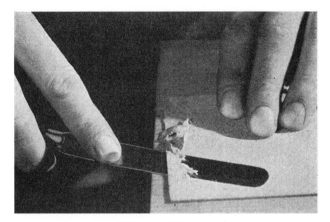

Fig. 24. Skiving.

SKIVING. Where two or more thicknesses of leather are to be put together, it is necessary to reduce the thickness of the edges.

To do this, the leather is placed on a smooth, solid surface, usually the cutting board. Place the skiving knife at the proper slope, and cutting back from the edge of the leather as far as desired, move the knife along smoothly and evenly as shown in Figure 24. The skiving knife must be kept very sharp.

APPLYING THE CEMENT. Leather cement is used around the edges to hold the lining in place during the lacing process. See Figure 25. The only kind of cement that will adhere to leather satisfactorily is a cement made especially for leather.

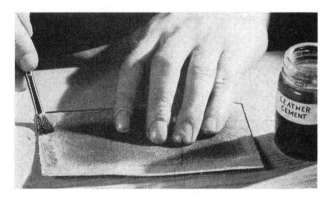

Fig. 25. Applying leather cement.

Fig. 26. Removing wrinkles with edge creaser.

PLACING THE LINING. The lining is usually cut slightly larger than the article to be lined. It is then placed upon the cemented surface and rubbed in all directions with the edge creaser or with a straight-edge piece of material, as shown in Figure 26, to remove wrinkles.

In order to *set* the lining to the leather, it is necessary to fold the material so that as many wrinkles as possible may be worked out before the project is laced. See Figure 27.

Fig. 27. Folding leather to remove wrinkles.

DYEING

Usually dye is employed to bring contrast into a background or to bring out certain types of design. No dye should be applied to a leather project until all the other processes of decoration have been completed.

KINDS OF DYES. Water dyes are perhaps the most simple and the most commonly used for coloring leather. They are purchased in powder form and dissolved in water. Instructions for mixing usually accompany the dyes, and they should be followed carefully. After the dyes are thoroughly dissolved, they may be applied with a soft camel's-hair brush.

PREPARING THE SURFACE. If the leather seems greasy or oily, it should first be cleaned with a solution of ammonia water. Then the entire surface of the leather should be moistened to check capillary action. This will keep the dye from spreading where it is not wanted. Be sure to permit each coat of dye to dry thoroughly before applying another. If there is any doubt as to the final color of the dye, one should experiment on a small piece of scrap leather before using it on the project.

The beginner must be careful when he is using dye, as it is almost impossible to remove it after it has been once applied.

Figure 28 shows a very satisfactory method of keeping dyes in order.

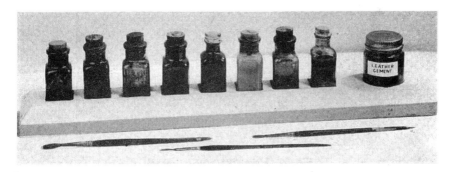

Fig. 28. Holder for dyes and leather cement.

APPLYING DYE. Small camel's-hair brushes give the most satisfactory results when applying dye. Great care should be given that the same brush is not used in different colored dyes. The brush should be cleaned by washing with soap and water after it has been used.

LACING

The general appearance of a project is affected very much by the kind of lacing that is applied. Good lacing is dependent upon the evenness of the lace in width, the spacing of the stitch, and the tension in the lace when the stitch is drawn. A little careful practice will enable any person to do a nice job of lacing.

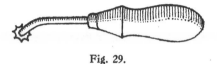

Fig. 29.

Figure 29 shows a spacing wheel which is used against the edge of a metal ruler. The points on the wheel determine the number of stitches, which are usually 6, 7, or 8 per inch. The ruler is usually placed ⅛ in. from the edge of the leather. Figure 30 shows how the spacing wheel is used.

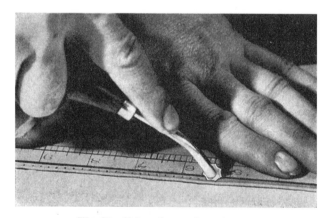

Fig. 30. Using the spacing wheel.

DIVIDER. When wide lace, such as Florentine lace, is to be used, the holes are spaced with a divider, such as is shown in Figure 31.

AWL. The awl is used for punching holes at the points made by the spacer. It should be held so as to punch the hole straight through the leather. See Figure 32.

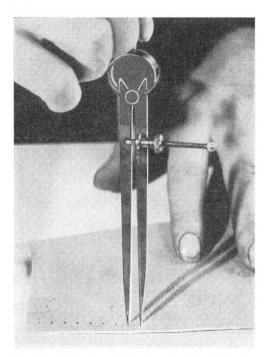

Fig. 31. Using the divider for locating the holes
for Florentine lace.

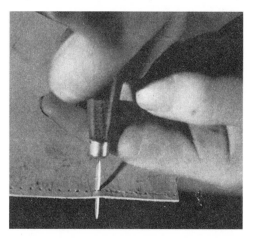

Fig. 32. Using the awl for making holes
for the lacing.

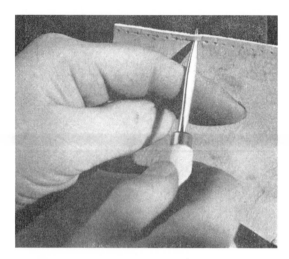

Fig. 34. Enlarging the awl holes with the fid.

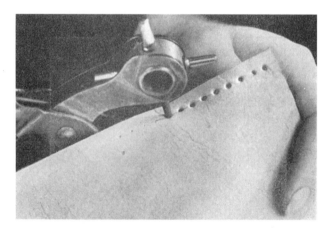

Fig. 36. Punching holes with the revolving punch.

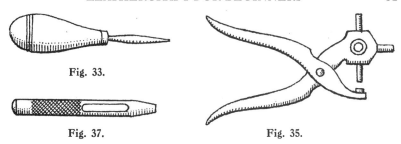

Fig. 33.

Fig. 37.

Fig. 35.

FID. The fid shown in Figure 33 is a tool which looks like an awl. It is used to enlarge the awl holes when the lace will not pass through readily. The fid should not be used to enlarge the holes too much, as they will then show, and the lacing will not have a neat appearance. Figure 34 shows how the fid is used.

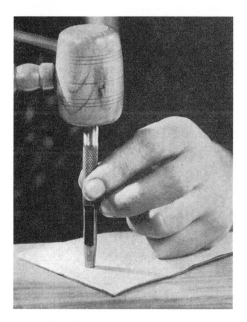

Fig. 38. Making a hole with
the drive punch.

REVOLVING PUNCH. The revolving punch, shown in Figure 35, is used for punching, for the wider lace such as is illustrated in Figure 41. It is used also for punching holes for snap fasteners, key posts, and the like.

A revolving punch is very practical because it will make many different-sized openings. Figure 36 pictures how a punch of this kind is used.

DRIVE PUNCH. When a drive punch, such as is shown in Figure 37, is used, the leather should be placed over a hardwood block. A wood mallet is then used to drive the punch through the leather. The mallet is preferable to a hammer, because with it the blow can be controlled more easily, and only sufficient force should be used to do the job intended.

The drive punch is used for punching larger holes, or for punching holes which cannot be reached with the revolving punch. See Figure 38.

METHOD OF LACING. There are different methods of lacing. Some leatherworkers lace away from themselves, as they hold the material in

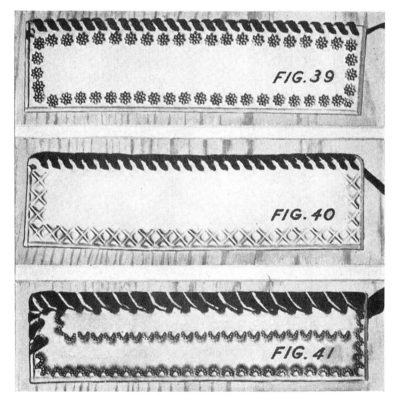

Fig. 39. Over-and-over lacing.
Fig. 40. Buttonhole lacing.
Fig. 41. Florentine lacing.

position, while others lace toward themselves. Professional leatherworkers use the method of lacing toward the person.

MAKING EVEN STITCHES. The secret of doing nice lacing is dependent upon the tension placed on the lace when the stitch is drawn. Even tension in every stitch makes an even stitch, and even stitches make an even edge.

HOW TO PREPARE THE END OF THE LACE. At times it is difficult to push the lace through the opening made by the awl. This may be overcome by cutting the lace so as to bring it out to a sharp point. Then apply a thin coat of shellac to make the lace rigid so it will pass through the opening easily. Needles made of split bamboo, to which the lace is glued, also may be used.

SPLICING THE LACE. In making the splice, where a new lace is to be added, the edges of the joining laces should be skived thin and cemented together with leather cement or with ambroid glue. When the new stitch is then started, the joined lace will not pull apart. The same procedure should be followed where the lacing is finished up.

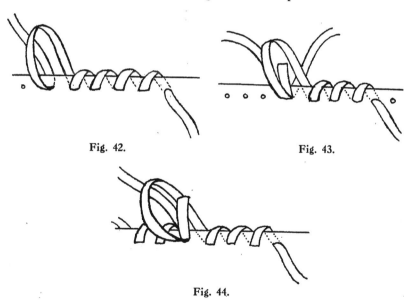

Fig. 42.   Fig. 43.

Fig. 44.

Lacing Stitches

Many different styles of stitches are used in lacing leather articles. Three of the most common ones are the *over-and-over stitch*, the *button-*

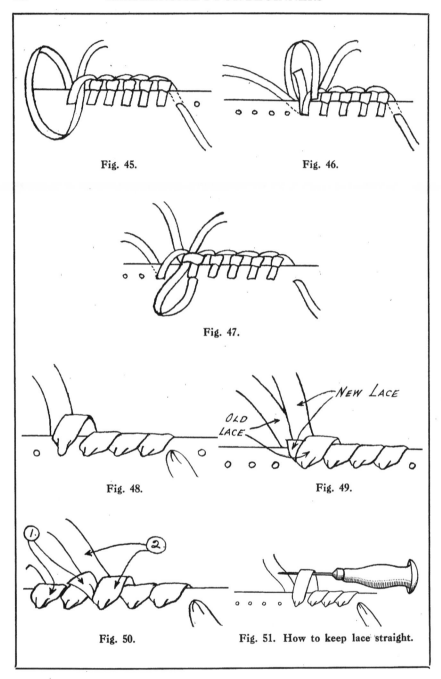

Fig. 45.   Fig. 46.

Fig. 47.

Fig. 48.   Fig. 49.

Fig. 50.   Fig. 51. How to keep lace straight.

hole stitch, and the *Florentine lace stitch.* Figures 39, 40, and 41 illustrate these three styles of lacing.

How to Estimate the Amount of Lace Needed. In using the *over-and-over* lacing stitch, the length of the lace needed will be three times the distance around the project. In using the *buttonhole stitch* the length of the lace needed will be five times the distance around the project.

Over-and-Over Stitch. This stitch is very simple. Hold the material in the left hand with the tooled side toward you. Insert the lace (with the rough side up), and simply whip over and over as shown in Figure 42. The splicing of the lace is shown in Figure 43, and Figure 44 illustrates how the two laces are joined in finishing the stitching.

Fig. 52. Using the burnisher.

Buttonhole Stitch. Hold the material in the left hand with the tooled side toward you. Push the lace through the hole made by the awl. Keep the rough side of the leather up. Study the procedure as shown in Figure 45. Figure 46 shows the method of splicing the lace. Skive the end of the new lace and glue to the edge under the new stitch. Figure 47 shows how to join the two laces when the stitching is finished.

Florentine Lace Stitch. Florentine lace is usually cut in widths varying from $\frac{1}{4}$ to $\frac{3}{8}$ in. The holes in the leather for the lacing are set apart a distance equal to the width of the lace. To make this stitch, bring the lace over and over as shown in Figure 48. The splicing of the two laces is shown in Figure 49, and the joining of the laces at the finish is shown in Figure 50. To do nice work, the lace must be made to lie

Fig. 53. Rubbing the lace with the mallet.

flat on the edge. This may be accomplished by drawing the lace over the awl, as shown in Figure 51, when the stitch is being made.

FINISHING

It is practically impossible to tool a leather project without causing minor defects, such as scratches, water spots, fingerprints, and the like. These imperfections cannot be removed entirely but much can be done

Fig. 54. Cleaning and polishing the leather.

to obliterate them. Great cleanliness and care to avoid scratches should be observed throughout the development of the project.

BURNISHER. A burnisher is used for removing scratches, dents, and the like. Figure 52 shows how the tool is used to rub the grain of the leather together so that the imperfections will not show.

SMOOTHING THE LACE. Much may be added to the appearance of the lace if the smooth side of the mallet is rubbed over the inner and outer surface of the lace in the direction taken by the slant of the stitch. Figure 53 shows how this is done. This process flattens the lace and *sets* the stitch to the openings made by the awl.

POLISHING is done to bring out the color and to protect the surface of the leather from moisture, scratches, finger marks, and the like. The writer thinks it best to buy the polishing materials especially prepared rather than try to make them. The polish may be applied with a soft cloth. After it has dried for a short time it may be polished with a block, covered with sheepskin, as shown in Figure 54.

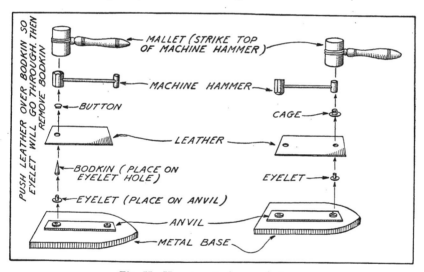

Fig. 55. How to attach snap fasteners.

ATTACHING SNAP FASTENERS

Snap fasteners are quite commonly used. They are used to hold down the flaps of coin purses, inside pocket flaps of billfolds, key cases, and in many other places. The procedure for attaching snap fasteners is illustrated in Figure 55.

ATTACHING KEY PLATES

Key plates are used on most types of key-case holders. The plates may be obtained with from two to six hooks. The procedure for attaching them with tubular rivets is illustrated in Figure 56. The center punch will expand the rivet head quite successfully. Of course, a tool specially designed for this purpose may also be obtained.

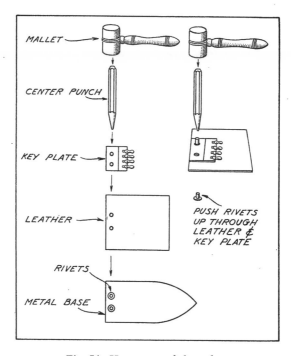

Fig. 56. How to attach key plate.

PROJECTS

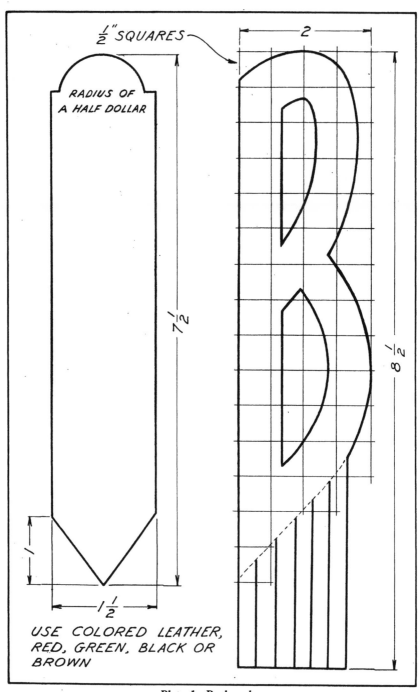

Plate 1. Bookmarks.

PROJECTS

Eleven projects are herewith submitted which will be of special interest to beginners. These projects involve the fundamental operations of leathercraft in logical sequence. Only a small amount of material is involved in each of the first eight projects. The student may elaborate on the designs used as his individual ability will permit.

A list of the materials needed has been given with each of the projects.

I. Bookmarks

Bookmarks, besides being useful, are very simple to make. It is possible to vary the design and to bring out individual expression of lines. The chief experience derived from this project is that of cutting. Plate 1 shows two designs that will serve very well.

MATERIAL

1 pc. calfskin ....1½ by 7½ in.
1 pc. calfskin ....2 by 8½ in.

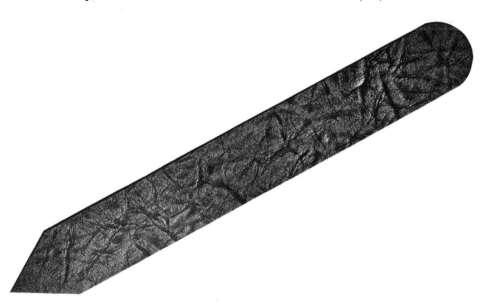

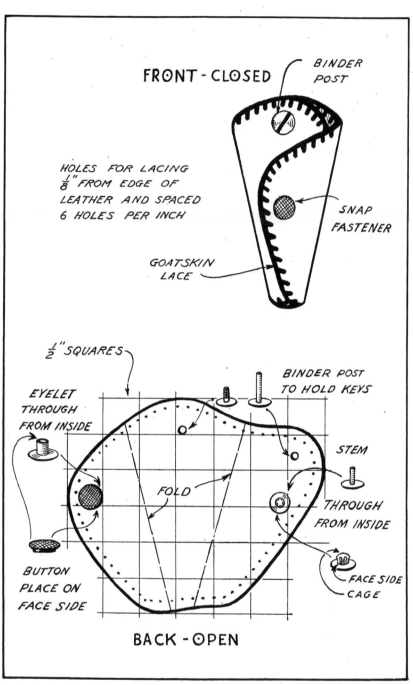

FRONT - CLOSED

BINDER POST

HOLES FOR LACING ⅛" FROM EDGE OF LEATHER AND SPACED 6 HOLES PER INCH

SNAP FASTENER

GOATSKIN LACE

½" SQUARES

BINDER POST TO HOLD KEYS

EYELET THROUGH FROM INSIDE

STEM

FOLD

THROUGH FROM INSIDE

BUTTON PLACE ON FACE SIDE

FACE SIDE CAGE

BACK - OPEN

Plate 2. Car-key case.

II. Car-Key Case

Plate 2 shows a car-key case which is very practical and useful. It is comparatively simple to make, involves many of the fundamental operations, and has a definite purpose when completed.

MATERIAL

1 pc. calf or steer hide.................3 by 3½ in.
Goatskin lace ....1½ yd.
1 complete snap fastener
1 binding post

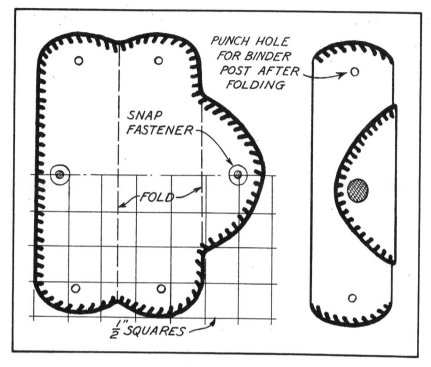

Plate 3. Double key holder.

III. Double Key Holder

The double key holder shown in Plate 3 is used by people who carry automobile keys. It may be used, also, for the keys of the home. It is a very popular project.

MATERIAL

1 pc. calf or steer hide.....................$3\frac{1}{2}$ by 4 in.
Goatskin lace...........................$2\frac{1}{4}$ yd.
1 complete snap fastener
2 binding posts

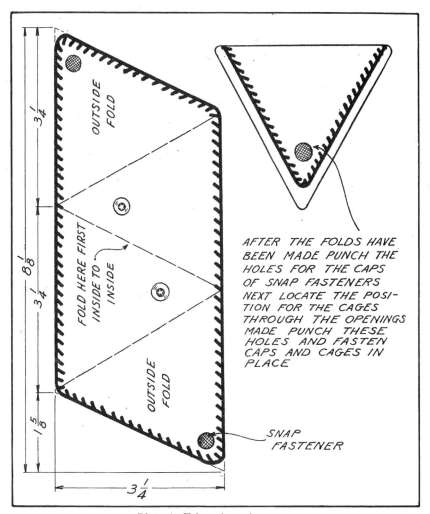

Plate 4. Triangular coin purse.

IV. Triangular Coin Purse

The triangular coin purse shown in Plate 4 is one of the most popular craftwork projects in camps. It is quite simple to make. Girls like to make it of colored leather.

MATERIAL

1 pc. calf or steer hide.................... 3¼ by 8 in.
Goatskin lace............................. 2½ yd.
2 complete snap fasteners

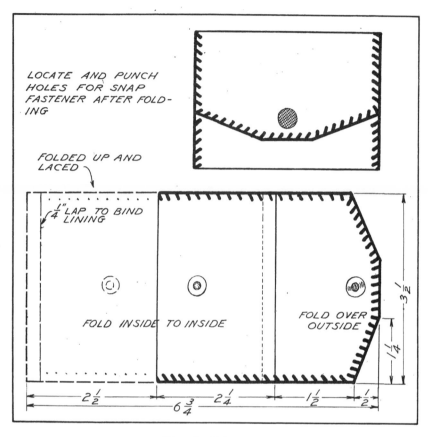

Plate 5. Coin purse.

V. Coin Purse

The purse shown in Plate 5 may be carried inside of a lady's handbag or it may be carried in the hand. It is the first project in the list to have a lining.

MATERIAL

1 pc. calf (if no lining is used) . . . . 3½ by 6½ in.
1 pc. steer hide (if lining is used) . . . . 3½ by 6¾ in.
1 pc. suede (for lining) . . . . 3½ by 6½ in.
Goatskin lace . . . . 2¼ yd.
1 complete snap fastener

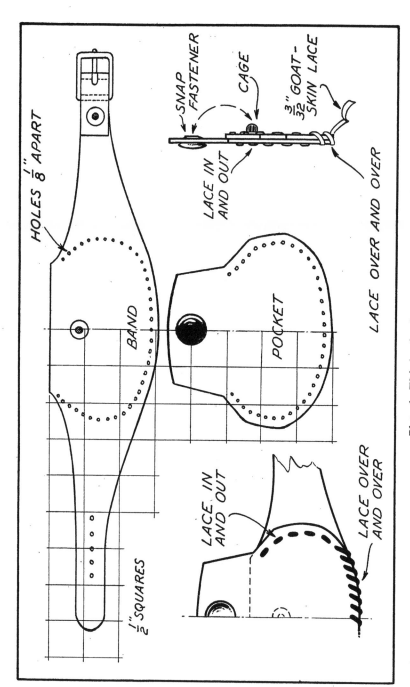

Plate 6. Wristband coin purse.

VI. Wristband Coin Purse

The wristband coin purse shown in Plate 6 is useful to boys and girls alike. It offers a safe way for them to carry their daily allowance in school and in camp. The project is very simple to make and involves only a small amount of material. Different colors of leather may be used to suit the tastes of the individual.

MATERIAL

1 pc. calfskin ....1¾ by 9   in.
1 pc. calfskin ....2¼ by 2½ in.
1/3-yd. goatskin lace....................3/32 in.
1 buckle
1 snap fastener
1 rapid rivet

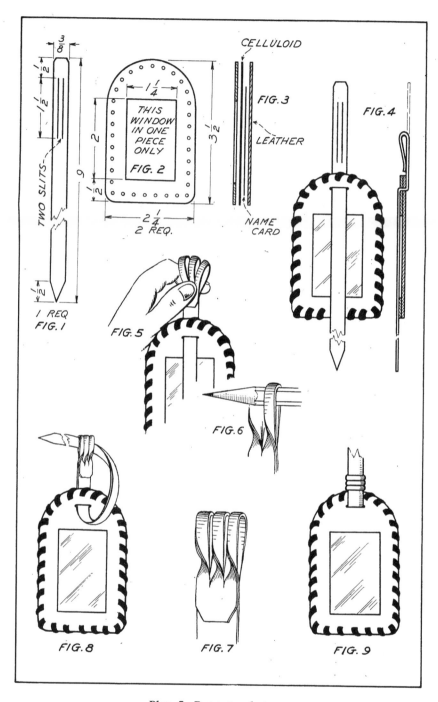

Plate 7. Bag tag and strap.

VII. Bag Tag and Strap

The bag tag shown in Plate 7 is commonly used by traveling people. It is rather easy to make and offers opportunity for some simple decorating with stamps. The different steps for attaching the holder strap is shown. Considerable care and accuracy is necessary if the finished article is to appear neat.

MATERIAL

2 pc. tooling calf or cowhide............2¼ by 3½ in.
1 pc. tooling calf or cowhide............ ⅜ by 9   in.
1 pc. celluloid ....2¼ by 3½ in.
Goatskin lace .... ¾ yd.

Since this particular project offers special difficulties, it was thought well to give step-by-step directions.

1. Cut tooling calf or cowhide to the shapes shown in Figures 1 and 2.

2. Place a piece of celluloid and a name card between the front and back as shown in Figure 3.

3. Lace the pieces together and insert the strap. Fold the end of the strap over. See Figure 4.

4. Separate the loops as shown in Figure 5.

5. Insert a pencil from the left side of each loop and give one-half twist as shown in Figure 6. See Figure 7 for finished result.

6. Insert the tapered end of the strap in loops as shown in Figure 8. Pull up tight. Figure 9 shows the strap attached to the back tag.

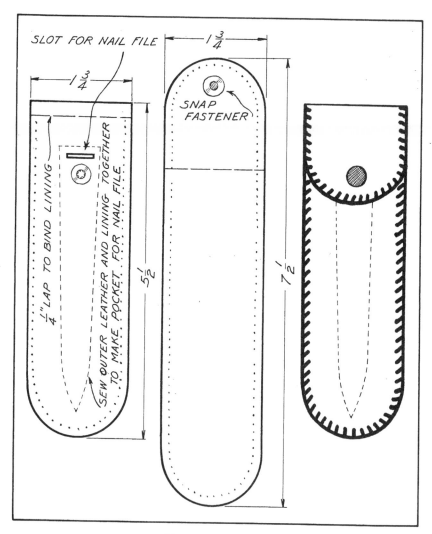

Plate 8. Comb case.

VIII. Comb Case

Boys take particular pride in making this practical project which is shown in Plate 8. A lining of thin calf adds much to the appearance. The holder for the nail file is made by sewing the outer leather and the lining together. It is necessary to make the opening for the stem of the snap fastener and to insert it before the lining is attached, or the project laced.

MATERIAL

1 pc. steer hide	1¾ by 7½ in.
1 pc. steer hide	1¾ by 5½ in.
1 pc. thin calf (lining)	1¾ by 7½ in.
Goatskin lace	2½ yd.
1 complete snap fastener	

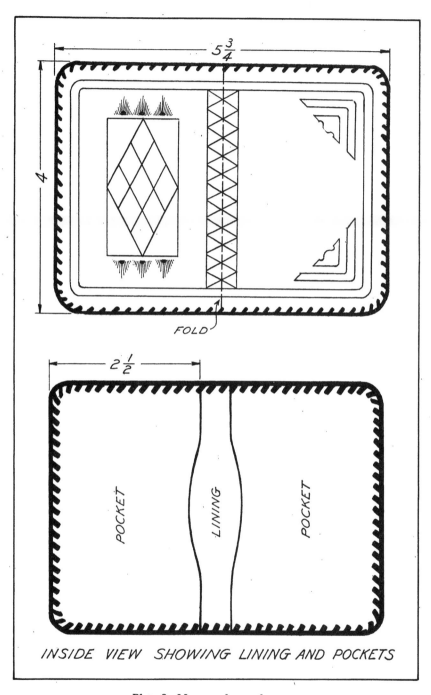

INSIDE VIEW SHOWING LINING AND POCKETS

Plate 9. Memorandum-pad cover.

IX. Memorandum-Pad Cover

The memorandum-pad cover shown in Plate 9 may be made to fit the small paper pads which may be purchased at any office supply house. It is simple to make and may be carried in a lady's handbag. A thin calf lining is used for an inside finish. The lining should be inserted after all the tooling is done. The inside pockets are cut and held in place by the outside lace.

MATERIAL

1 pc. steer hide 4   by 5¾ in.
2 pc. steer hide (inside pockets)..........2½ by 4   in.
1 pc. thin calf 4   by 5¾ in.
Goatskin lace ....3 yd.

Plate 10. Belts.

X. Belt

Boys and girls, alike, enjoy making belts. Much individuality may be shown in their construction, and they may utilize either stamped or tooled designs. See the different types of ornamentation shown in Plate 10. The buckle on all belts should be laced on, or attached with two snap fasteners. The loop for the end to be pushed through should be fastened in place by one or two stitches. The length of the belt may be determined by taking the individual's waist measure. This should always be done when ordering belt material.

MATERIAL

1 pc. steer hide or cowhide . . . . 1½ by 32 in.
Goatskin lace . . . . 1 yd.
1½-in. buckle (flat)

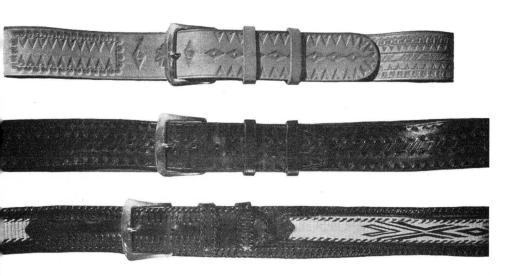

Plate 11. Book cover.

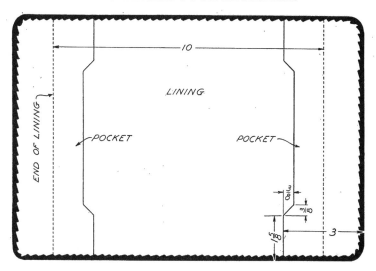

Lining book covers.

XI. Book Cover

Two designs of book covers are shown in Plate 11. One is an Indian design and the other is suitable for a monogram. To develop the project a full-sized paper pattern should be made. Every detail should be included in the pattern so that it may be transferred to the leather for tooling. Thin calf or suede should be used for the lining. Florentine lace is most suitable for this type of project.

MATERIAL

1 pc. steer or calf .... 8¾ by 13   in.
2 pc. steer or calf (inside pockets) 3   by 8¾ in.
1 pc. thin calf or suede lining .... 8¾ by 13   in.
Florentine lace ⅜ in. wide .... 5 yd.

SUGGESTED MONOGRAM DESIGNS

Plate 12.

Monogram Designs

Monograms are suitable for many different types of projects. They add a personal value to the article when completed. The style of the monogram may be made or designed to fit the project. The designs shown in Plates 12 and 13, present various ideas as to how monograms may be developed. Nicely tooled monograms give a striking appearance to the finished project.

Plate 14 shows appropriate designs which are suitable for many types of projects. They may be tooled rather easily and made to appear quite effective. The designs shown are typical of those commonly used.

RCC

RCC

H.L.B

SUGGESTED MONOGRAM DESIGNS

Plate 13.

Plate 14. Suggested designs which may be adapted to various projects.